Rosa Parks

by Wil Mara

Content Consultant
Nanci R. Vargus, Ed.D.
Professor Emeritus, University of Indianapolis

Reading Consultant
Jeanne Clidas, Ph.D.
Reading Specialist

Children's Press®
An Imprint of Scholastic Inc.
New York Toronto London Auckland Sydney
Mexico City New Delhi Hong Kong
Danbury, Connecticut

Library of Congress Cataloging-in-Publication Data
Mara, Wil.
Rosa Parks/by Wil Mara; poem by Jodie Shepherd. — [Revised edition].
    pages cm. — (Rookie biographies)
Includes bibliographical references and index.
ISBN 978-0-531-20561-7 (library binding: alk. paper) — ISBN 978-0-531-21204-2 (pbk.: alk. paper)
    1. Parks, Rosa, 1913-2005—Juvenile literature. 2. African Americans—
Alabama—Montgomery—Biography—Juvenile literature. 3. African American
women—Alabama—Montgomery—Biography—Juvenile literature. 4. Civil rights
workers—Alabama—Montgomery—Biography—Juvenile literature. 5. African
Americans—Civil rights—Alabama—Montgomery—History—20th century—Juvenile
literature. 6. Segregation in transportation—Alabama—Montgomery—History—20th
century—Juvenile literature. 7. Montgomery (Ala.)—Race relations—Juvenile
literature. I. Shepherd, Jodie. II. Title.

F334.M753P38554 2014
323.092—dc23 [B]   2014015416

Produced by Spooky Cheetah Press
Poem by Jodie Shepherd
Design by Keith Plechaty

© 2015 by Scholastic Inc.

Photographs © 2015: Alamy Images/age fotostock: 27; AP Images: 8, 15, 31 top
(Gene Herrick), 4, 30 top left (Khue Bui), 30 top right (Richard Sheinwald); Corbis
Images/Bettmann: cover, 23; Getty Images: 3 bottom (Bill Pugliano), 16, 12, 19, 20,
31 center top (Don Cravens/Time Life Pictures), 28 (Paul Sancya/AFP), 24 (Richard
Ellis/AFP), 11, 31 bottom (Stan Wayman//Time Life Pictures), 3 top right (United States
Postal Service), 3 top left, 31 center bottom (Universal History Archive).

Maps by XNR Productions, Inc.

Table of Contents

Rosa Parks

Meet Rosa Parks

Rosa Parks was an ordinary woman who did something extraordinary. On December 1, 1955, she refused to give up her seat on a city bus. This simple act of **defiance** helped launch the Civil Rights Movement in the United States. Today, Rosa is remembered as a true hero.

Rosa was born on February 4, 1913, in Tuskegee, Alabama. She went to schools that were for African-American students only. **Segregation** laws also kept black people out of some restaurants, stores, and other places.

FAST FACT!

Rosa had to leave high school to care for her sick mother and grandmother. She later went back to get her diploma.

Tennessee

NC

Miss.

Georgia

Alabama

Tuskegee ●

Florida

MAP KEY

Alabama

● Town where
Rosa Parks
was born

Gulf of Mexico

7

8

When Rosa was 19, she met Raymond Parks and the two married. They settled in Montgomery, Alabama.

In 1943, Rosa joined the National Association for the Advancement of Colored People (NAACP). Soon she became secretary to the president, E.D. Nixon. She also worked in a store.

Rosa is walking into the courthouse with E.D. Nixon.

Rosa rode a city bus to and from work. Black people could sit only in certain seats. These seats were toward the back of the bus. If all the "white" seats were full, black passengers had to give up their seats and stand. If there was no place to stand, black people had to get off the bus.

In the South, black people had to sit toward the back of city buses.

11

12

Trouble on the Bus

On December 1, 1955, Rosa boarded a bus after work. She sat in a seat behind the "black" section sign.

As the bus filled up with white passengers, the driver moved the sign back. He told Rosa and three other people to give up their seats. Rosa refused.

13

This photo shows Rosa getting fingerprinted after her arrest. ▶

The police took Rosa to the police station. She was charged with breaking one of Montgomery's segregation laws. Rosa was put in a jail cell until some friends came to **bail** her out.

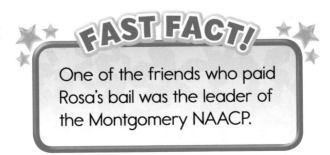

FAST FACT!

One of the friends who paid Rosa's bail was the leader of the Montgomery NAACP.

Boycott!

After Rosa's arrest, black people in the area were asked to **boycott** all Montgomery buses. A young minister named Martin Luther King Jr. was chosen to lead the bus boycott.

Martin Luther King Jr. planned the boycott with members of the NAACP.

The Montgomery Bus Boycott began on Monday, December 5. Thousands of people stayed off the buses. They found other ways to get around town. The bus companies lost a lot of money. Finally, after 381 days, Montgomery got rid of its busing segregation laws.

Many black people walked to work rather than take the bus.

19

After the boycott, black people could sit in any seat on the bus.

The boycott was a huge victory for the Civil Rights Movement. But for Rosa and her husband, it was the beginning of a very hard time. They both lost their jobs and were unable to find new ones. In 1957, they moved out of Alabama. They later settled in Detroit, Michigan.

Civil Rights Leader

The Civil Rights Movement continued to grow. In 1964, President Lyndon B. Johnson signed the Civil Rights Act. It ended segregation at work, at restaurants, at stores, and at other public places.

Rosa continued to work for equality for African Americans.

23

<figure>24</figure>

In 1987, Rosa founded the Rosa and Raymond Parks Institute for Self Development. It teaches young people how to reach their life goals. She also received many awards. In 1996, President Clinton presented her with the Presidential Medal of Freedom. In 1999, she received the Congressional Gold Medal.

FAST FACT!

Rosa wrote a book for young people called *My Story*, and another about her religious faith called *Quiet Strength*.

Rosa died on October 24, 2005. She was 92 years old. Her coffin was put in the United States Capitol Building in Washington, D.C. It was a great honor. More than 50,000 people came to say good-bye.

FAST FACT!

Rosa is called "the Mother of the Civil Rights Movement."

Capitol Building

27

Vice President Al Gore

Timeline of Rosa Parks's Life

1932
marries Raymond Parks

1913
born on February 4

1955
arrested on December 1;
Montgomery Bus Boycott begins

Rosa believed that America should be a land of equality for all people. She forever changed the course of history and is a hero to millions of people.

1956
boycott ends; Alabama desegregates public buses

1999
receives Congressional Gold Medal

1987
founds the Rosa and Raymond Parks Institute for Self Development

2005
dies on October 24

A Poem About
Rosa Parks

Quietly, without a fuss,

she took a seat inside the bus,

which helped to end—across the nation—

the unfair laws of segregation.

You Can Be
Courageous

- Be willing to work for change if you believe that change is for the better.

- Work hard at something if you believe it is right, even if others try to stop you.

- Always treat people the way you would like to be treated. Expect the same in return.

Glossary

bail (bayl): amount of money paid to get someone out of jail

boycott (BOY-kot): refusal to use a product or a service

defiance (di-FYE-unhts): standing up to a person or an organization

segregation (seg-ruh-GAY-shuhn): separating people of different races within a society

Index

Facts for Now

Visit this Scholastic Web site for more information on Rosa Parks:
www.factsfornow.scholastic.com
Enter the keywords **Rosa Parks**

About the Author

Wil Mara is the award-winning author of more than 140 books. Many are educational titles for children.